# Smell of Earth and Clay
## East Greenland Songs

Translated by Lawrence Millman

# WHITE PINE PRESS

ISBN-0-934834-54-7

Published by White Pine Press
73 Putnam Street
Buffalo, New York 14213

# Introduction

Eric the Red and his son Leif. Vanished Norsemen. The whaling trade. Smiling Eskimo hunters. The unsmiling Thule air base. Ice-houses and women perfumed with seal fat. Moravian Brethren instructing the locals that it's wrong to kill a new-born girl-child or send off the aged and infirm to wander the icy wastes.

Such are the scenes and images inspired by the word "Greenland." They come to us from *West* Greenland, which has long been accessible to the public mind. The East is a somewhat different matter because of the huge masses of ice blocking its coast and clogging its fjords. The eternal procession of this ice kept Europeans at bay until 1822 when William Scoresby the Younger (whose father, the Elder, invented the "crow's nest") mapped eight hundred miles of eastern coastline. Scoresby discovered abandoned camps and old utensils, but did not see a living soul. On August 17, 1823, Captain Douglas Charles Clavering penetrated Gael Hamke's Bay and encountered a tribe of twelve Eskimos living in a single tent. They disappeared without a trace after Clavering showed them how to use firearms. Even today there are stories of a Stone Age tribe which lives somewhere in the Northeast, retreating to the Ice Cap when they sense they're about to be "discovered." Abandoned camps have been found, discarded utensils, fires . . .

The outside world gained its first real glimpse of the Eastlanders in 1884 when Captain Gustav Holm of the Danish Navy sailed around Cape Farewell and headed north in search of the lost Norse colony, which he thought might have survived in some lonely eastern fjord. Instead, Holm discovered the legendary Angmagssalimiut at their settlement of Angmagssalik. This community, which numbered only 416, had never seen a white man before. They took Holm and his crew to be the offspring of a woman of their tribe who long ago had mated with a dog. There were many stories and songs about this mating, about other matings, and about everything else from the origin of the earth to the omnipotence of lice. For the arts flourished in this corner of the globe.

Yet the Angmagssalik people were suffering a lengthy apocalypse at the time of Holm's visit. Winters had become more and more violent and there was such a scarcity of food that quite a few people had recently committed suicide rather than starve to death. Women were becoming barren. Cannibalism was not uncommon. Just two years before, only two people of an outlying depot of nineteen had survived the winter, and they had done so only by eating the flesh of their dead. A woman named Keligasak had eaten her husband, eight of her children, and four grandchildren.

Danish beneficence may have saved them from extinction. By 1895, a trading post had been set up in Angmagssalik. The people were provided with steel tools and firearms, the better to hunt the seal. That universal panacea, tobacco, seems to have relieved at least some of their distress—they cut it with quartz to make it last longer. They adapted well to the age of machines. Nowadays the grandsons of these desperate people repair refractory motors and pilot helicopters. A town has grown up where the old trading post used to be. And a D.E.W. installation squats at Kulusuk, not far from where Keligasak ate three generations of her family.

Exactly one hundred years after Gustav Holm, I paid a visit to Angmagssalik. The town reminded me of many other outposts of the Arctic. It was situated on a steepdown hillside and seemed ready at any moment to plunge into the sea. The rocky soil yielded only cans of beer. Sled dogs howled at each other all night long . . . quite a pleasant music, really. One bright midnight I walked down to the pier and met a hunter who was flensing a seal. His name was Ib Brodersen. I asked him for a bite of raw seal liver, a delicacy finer to my mind than the very best steak. Whereupon he offered me a piece at the end of his knife, saying, "You should wash that down with a vintage Beaujolais . . ."

For all his European leanings, Ib Brodersen came fully equipped with the legacy of his people. He turned out to be an even greater repository of old songs than he was of liquor. Soon I had recorded a number of these songs. Later, in a surreal duet of English, Greenlandic, and Danish, we worked over their meanings. I obtained more songs from Ib's brother-in-law, a catechist, and from an early collection put together by William Thalbitzer. And seated on a rock high above the icebergs of

Angmagssalik Fjord, I started to render this bounty into English.

The songs of East Greenland contain certain traditional Eskimo elements along with a grotesquerie that is decidedly local. "Song for a New Wife," for instance, exists in variants throughout the Polar North. As the people of the east coast occasionally traded with West Greenlanders, it may have arrived in a kayak laden with skins and furs. But I doubt that "The Barren Woman's Lament" could be from anywhere but the east of Greenland. If you suffered through the famine years of the last century, you too might love a worm. You might also ask a raven for the human thigh-bone in his beak so that your children will have something to gnaw upon ("The Raven").

Above all, these songs—whether migratory or local—are heroic testimony to the power of poetry to break through even the most desolate of circumstances. They give the lie to W. H. Auden's remark that poetry makes nothing happen. An Angmagssalimiut's song was designed to raise the dead; to protect a child from pain and injury; to prevent an avalanche; to capture a seal; and to capture a woman as well. His word for "song" is the same as his word for "breath" (and breathing, as we all know, is rather important). Poetry only makes nothing happen in the parlors of academe; and it especially makes nothing happen during the occasion known as a "poetry reading," which seldom if ever brings about good hunting or halts the progress of an avalanche.

Anonymity is the price of being human. No one really knows who composed these songs. The death of the song-maker casts the shadow of taboo over his name; after death, that name cannot be uttered. Thus Fame, as it falls to the likes of a Lowell or a Berryman, never falls to the Greenlander. Probably Fame would matter to him much less than a nice fat bearded seal. In the absence of this seal, I offer you these songs . . .

Lawrence Millman
*Angmagssalik—Cambridge, Massachusetts*

O rich summer warmth
like the flesh of a woman
O sparkling day
neither clouds or wind
and in the blue mountains
a herd of reindeer
grazing in the blue distance
O how it touches me
so miraculous
I lie down on the ground, sobbing

# The Salmon

*Aja*, look at that salmon there
it's shaped like a fat penis
with a belly full of roe
look at its fat dorsal fin
look at its fat back
look at its fat belly
look at that fat salmon there
and what a pity
I've forgotten my harpoon

# Song of the Ptarmigan

Behold the feathery person
who struts there in the new snow
He's sniffing out a mate
he's got red eyelids
a white jerkin
big stomach
What wonderful guts!
But his moist little ass
behold there!      so sweet
the entry and exit of his soul

My woman touches me between the legs
she gives me her body
*Aja*, she rips the leather bracelets
off my wrists

# Drum-Song Against an Angry Husband

My enemy calls me a cannibal
he says I feed on human flesh
my friends, that's not true
my enemy calls me a thief
he says I stole his dear wife
my friends, I did steal her
and it was not wrong to do so
for I am the better singer
and he did not have songs to keep her
only now does he sing about her
when he never praised her before
never once sang lovely songs to her
who cried in her tent all alone
My friends, she is my wife now

# Isserfik

There lived a young girl named Isserfik
O she was a fine piece of blubber
There lived a young girl named Isserfik
and he who saw her loved her
O Isserfik, why don't you fancy me?
Because I fancy eagles more, she'd say
Give me an eagle over a man any day
Now there was an eagle from Qassiasut
and it seems he fancied her rather well
he came and carried her to the North
and in his nest together they lay
It was only magic that called her back
the *angakok* cast a ferocious spell
that struck dead this eagle from the North
and brought home his wife, her belly a-swell
O Isserfik, what't that in your amaut sack?
It's the beautiful little girl I've hatched
half-human, half-eagle
and dearly do I love her
Ah, Isserfik used to be a fine piece of blubber

# Song for a New Wife

My wife, my dear wife
wipe away your tears
for this island is your home now
the best island in the world
here you will have suet to eat
tasty suet
you will have tender whale meat
and seal eyes, luscious seal eyes
the best seal eyes in the whole world

# Amulet Charm for a Pregnant Woman

Enter me, O little amulet stone
the path is smooth and easy
                        into my womb
be my fetus, O round little stone
it's very nice in there
                        no blood at all
creep into my inside
                        my new stone-child
that the other child
                        kicking at me
that this other child
                        growing in me
may soon see his father

# The Barren Woman's Lament

Because I could not get with child
I went around in sorrow
Because I could not get with child
I paid a visit to some worms
and because I could not get with child
I took home a sweet little worm
This worm I wrapped in a skin-stocking
this worm I lay against my breast
and there it grew fat, oh so fat
my own suckling babe
and I grew lean
You're a bag of bones, said my husband
your greedy child is eating you alive
and he cut my dear one into small pieces
which he fed to the dogs
It is not a good thing, my friends
not a good thing at all to love a worm

# Cradle Song

Cry not, my little one
cry not
else a large raven will pick out your eyes
a large raven will pick out your eyes
my dear sweet little one

# Lullaby

my dear little plague
all you want is my milk
you'll drink me dry
forever sucking
sucking at my dugs
like when you were born
as you sucked then
so you suck now
big strong healthy child
whose ass is so hot
it burns me

# Petting Song

Riding high, the little flirt
in the amaut on my back
No man has yet touched her
no man has yet stamped her
no man has yet cleaved her
But it's not her fault
Look how her eyes follow men
She runs after every man she sees
All she wants is a man
      my little child

Greedy snowslide
keep your paws off my little house
I've got a wife and four kids
they could never gratify you
like they gratify me

Strong snowslide
if you must flex your muscles
kindly smash a few rocks
bury a cliff-side or two
but don't touch this little house of mine

I know, O snowslide
that I built my house on your land
but where else could I find shelter
from your comrade the wind?
Where else but in your lap?

Generous snowslide
my wife and kids are all I have
it wouldn't amuse you to kill them
let them sleep in peace
Stay up there on your nice cold mountain

# Hunter's Charm for the Prevention of an Avalanche

My grandfather and great-grandfather
and great-great-grandfather
all bade me come to this bird-cliff
therefore, you rocks, stay put

When friend Maaitak takes a new wife
I think I'll steal his old one
the great, delightful Big Vulva Woman
she of the great, delightful kisses
she of the mighty and everlasting kisses
*Aja*, even the lips of my ass
form the shape of a kiss now

# Against the Effects of Shooting Stars

Shooting star in the sky
ill rains fall on earth
Quick! a chunk of mica
and hide here under this moss
else the star-shit'll get us

# Sledge Song

Onward
sledge, glider, beast of burden
onward, onward
your fat thighs must grow slim

# Signal Song

From the kayak to the shore:

Of my prey
I sing
we met in the northland
we drove each other yet farther north
together we hunted
but I was better
I sang my lullaby to him
and he slept like the sea
A bear
a great bear I have brought home from the north
    and life is just fine

# Spell for Catching a Bearded Seal

What smell
do I smell of?
Of the smell of a bearded seal
the smell of earth and clay

# Walrus Hunter's Charm

Friend walrus, let me harpoon you
let me harpoon you by petting your jowls
such beautiful jowls
Now won't you be quiet?
Friend walrus, let me harpoon you
let me harpoon you by fondling your tusks
such delicate tusks
Now won't you be meek?

# Flensing Song

I put my knife to this bearded seal
I slit it open
I pull out the liver
and offer it to my husband
*Aja*, we are a joyful couple again

# Bad Hunter's Drum-Song

Why am I such a good-for-nothing?
What's the reason?
I can't beget a child
Perhaps it's because my penis is small
All my huntings are small too
I'll make a song about these huntings
It will be a small song
I'll begin with the ice-floes
one day I was paddling among them
I was paddling happily among them
when I saw an enormous Greenland seal
asleep, fast asleep on the ice
*Aja*, I stabbed him with my harpoon
and into the water he plunged
deep, deep into the water
I lost my bone-point in that seal
the bone-point of my harpoon
and I haven't been any good since then
either at hunting or anything else
*Aja*, my penis is so small

# Kulusuk Hunter's Song

Though my home place is nothing but slush
though I am drifting hopelessly on this floe of ice
though all I see is ice everywhere
though my belly is empty
*Aja*, I am full of joy

# The Raven

—Raven, raven
 what's that in your beak?
—A human thigh-bone
 so sweet, so sweet to eat
—Raven, raven
 give me a little piece
—But such a thigh-bone
 is better for ravens to eat
—Raven, raven
 my children need some food
—And my children, O man
 they're very hungry, too

# Kuk-ook's Song

A nasty little person am I
and I'm going to run away from home
to find some girl with a big vulva
and when I'm done with her
I'll feed her flesh to the sea-gulls
and come back to this pit
and throw a party for my dumb cousins
it'll be a very jolly party
I'll whip them to shreds with my rope
and feed their flesh to the gulls too
then I'll marry two girls at once
the first of my sweethearts
I'll dress in the finest spotted sealskins
and my other pet
she'll wear lovely skins of the hooded seal

# Young Girl's Lament

My parents, they've been rather cruel
they strapped me to our hut
and let the dogs gnaw at my knees
and left me in the snow and cold
all because I would not marry
But I chewed loose my bindings
Ah, said my father, You've done well
for a stupid girl who will not marry
Then he hung me head downwards
in a deep mountain ravine
to let the winds play at my skin
To these empty spaces I give this song:
I am far from happy hanging here
My lungs seem to fall in my eyes
My liver, it sleeps with my hair
my kidneys press against my nostrils
my guts are like an amaut string
and my heart sits heavily between my ears
and all because I will not marry

# Lament of the Snow Bunting

Listen to me, my poor husband:
the human beings are greater than us
and they are clever, too
they can make things with their hands
whale-bone snares, for example
it was in just such a snare
of bone and hair
that they grabbed your little life
Listen, O my poor husband:
after they stole your breath from you
they drowned our nest
and all our children
with their human piss
O my poor dead husband:
they must be truly great
who can make such a mighty piss

*Aja*, I'm a woman who never spawned a bastard
I'm a woman who never spawned a bastard
    *Aja*, I'm a fine big woman
    who is every man's toy
and I never, never spawned a bastard

with what lungs
            do I breathe?
with the lungs
            of a little butterfly
            I breathe
O how strong I am now
for Asiartik
            the wolf
            the devourer
            the bringer of sickness
Asiartik hates butterflies

# Charm Against Sickness

White gull
who soars over my dismal body
I'm talking to you, bird
Come down here
and grasp me with your wings
Let me fly in the blue air, too

# Charm Against Pain

What lives here inside me?
What sort of fetus?
The great inland ice lives here
and it hurts me greatly
What sort of fetus hurts my insides?
The great inland ice
and may these words melt it

# Old Woman's Song

How long will it last
                    this nasty old age
how long will the eyes of my people
                    scorn me
I draw my breath like a heavy stone
There is a fire in my chest
I can hardly hear my people
                    nor they hear me
Once I could bone and cut
                    the flesh of a great walrus
I had the quickest knife of any woman
Once I had no rival
                    flensing a seal
Now they think it's a waste
even to offer me
                    a nice bite of seal liver
they give me mussels instead

*Aja*, I've grown old
lived quite long enough
much wisdom I've acquired
but four riddles are beyond me

what made the sun
what made the moon
what made the minds of women
and why do people have so many lice

# Narwhal Song

Old worn-out eyes
old worn-out eyes
you will never see again
a run of narwhals
break the waves of the sea

I will call up the souls
of the narwhals I killed
perhaps their sweet souls
will brighten
my old worn-out eyes

I will make a song about them
they'll swim in my song
great herds of narwhals
who broke the foam
close to my village

Now I can see them lolling
and now spouting in the sea
herd after herd of narwhals
they bring back my youth
they give me this song

# For Raising the Dead

What am I bringing alive?
A dungfly I'm bringing alive
What am I bringing alive?
A butterfly I'm bringing alive
What am I bringing alive?
A wheatear I'm bringing alive
What am I bringing alive?
A fox I'm bringing alive
What am I bringing alive?
A crested seal I'm bringing alive
What am I bringing alive?
My father I'm bringing alive

# Mourning Song

No hunting
in this land
no hunting
on this ice
no hunting
in this air
no hunting
in this sea
no hunting at all

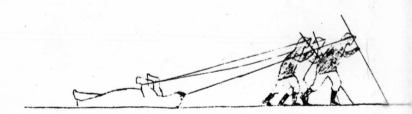